Sheltered
and
Before the Contagious

Sheltered
and
Before the Contagious

Cari Griffo

Poetry Factory
300 8th Ave. Suite 5G
Brooklyn, NY 11215

Published by Poetry Factory
300 8th Ave. Suite 5G
Brooklyn, NY 11215

ISBN 978-0-9762603-2-5

Cover Art and Design by Trent Edwards.

Typesetting services by BOOKOW.COM

To all those who suffered from the pandemic.

To Trent and Willa for whom I sheltered with, for whom I love deeply and grow the most with.

To all my family and friends who received a short poem a day in your inbox, I love you.

Acknowledgements

For the printed word or the spoken word:

"Dear Apple Tree," *Libros Press*, Spring 2021.

"December 26th, 2004," *Santa Fe New Music, composed by John Kennedy for Words on Water*, 2009.

"Swimmer," *Santa Fe New Music, composed by John Kennedy for Words on Water*, 2009.

"Cello Solo, To The Soul," *Santa Fe New Music, composed by John Kennedy for Words on Water*, 2009.

"Holy Water," *Manorborn*, Vol. 7, No.1, September 2009.

"Holy Water," *Telepoem Booth Santa Fe, NM*, 2019.

"Premonition," *Premonition, an original art book by Karla Winterowd and Cari Griffo*, 1998.

"Timing," *Timing, an original art book by Karla Winterowd and Cari Griffo*, 1998.

"Almost," *Almost, an original art book by Karla Winterowd and Cari Griffo*, 1998.

Thanks to my Mom and Dad who created a poet from inception.

Thanks to my family and friends who have inspired the muse, who have forced me to grow, who have helped me to see…yes, you.

Thank you, Gary, my fellow poet, my dear friend, you have encouraged me all the way.

Thanks to my two, one and only, Trent and Willa.

Audiences who have showed up to not only my poetry shows, but to all poetry events, you are necessary, a life-giving force for which I am forever fueled.

Tons of appreciation to Poetry Factory; wishing you an empire bigger than chocolate with poetry Oompa Loompas taking over the world.

The utmost gratitude is extended to all the recipients of A Poem a Day While Sheltered at Home email list.

Contents

Before the Contagious

"There is only one home to the life of a river-mussel; there is only one home to the life of a tortoise; there is only one shell to the soul of man: there is only one world to the spirit of our race. If that world leaves its course and smashes on boulders of the great void, whose world will give us shelter?"

Wole Soyinka

SHELTERED

INTRODUCTION

A simple thought one day during quarantine, to send my loved ones a little poem, a small gift to let them know I was thinking of them turned into, A Short Poem a Day While Sheltered at Home. After I placed my poem in the body of the email my curser hovered in the subject line as I searched for its words. Much like the muse which spurs the uncensored brainstorm, "A Short Poem" was typed in before I understood its meaning. I had no idea what I meant by "A Day," how many I would write/send, or what the content of "Sheltered" would feel like. The second day, and then the next, another new poem sent, the responses from family and friends were beyond appreciation; I received anything from poetry to personal stories in return.

A funny thing happened with the fifteenth poem, which at the time, was humiliating. Instead of sending to my Short Poem A Day list, by mistake, I sent the deeply sorrowful poem "Tulips 1" to my entire email list. Immediately, my fear wondered to the inboxes of my daughter's high school principal, to New Mexico's state auditor, to past employees of my husband's defunct business, to….to….to…..too many people I was sure a poem would not be wanted, and in this case, upon reading, could be disturbing.

I surmised many scenarios for solutions, however, I decided to let the email ride itself out by not doing anything, to wait and see. New responses came in to thank me, in which, I offered a brief explanation of what happened. I did not offer for them to be on the poetry list, as I thought it would be awkward to put them on the spot. However, many volunteered their own requests to be included in the daily emails. It was surprising to learn who surfaced as appreciators, hence, growing the Short Poem a Day list.

On day thirty-one, after writing 30 ("Expecting" was a re-write) new poems, the thirty-first short poem would be the last, the same way the first began, with no idea of its ending. The following is the final message I sent:

> I've decided yesterday to be the last day for these poetry emails. There was a total of 31 poems in which I thank you

for. Creating, while sheltered at home has been an incredible process, one in which, feels natural for a writer. However, the company you have provided me with during what would be a solitary practice has made these daily poems unique. I have brought the awareness of you, for whom I wrote for, into my living room. The pieces have humbled me as I have been less focused on their perfection with edits and more interested in releasing them to you as daily gifts.

Little could any of us have realized how this time would deepen our connections to what we value the most and to whom we treasure the most. This daily practice has kept me in communication with you and for this I am grateful. There have been so many unexpected responses, some of which include poems written back to me. You have opened my heart and given me the incentive to create out of love on behalf of love which is everlasting. I wish you all endurance, wellness, and peace.

And most of all, LOVE,

Cari

With love and gratitude to you, the reader, as you are now added to A Short Poem a Day While Sheltered at Home list. The poems appear in the same order as they were sent.

Love,
Cari

Sparrow

Sparrow is one sound
removed from sorrow
before she sings.

Eighteen

You are a high wind
on a spring day
howling
between walls
which should be the sound
of tires burning.

Facetime
cannot satiate
the speed of your yearning
for fingertips
meeting the skin
of another, your giggles
gust like the verdant
colors of a new earth.

Bathroom Plans

Our conversation starts
with the lighting
but goes straight
    to the electric.
We are sparking
    deep down
to the fuse box
where all shorts live,
and if we don't flip
    the switches
we run the risk
of a new soffit
    housing
explosive bulbs.

DEAR APPLE TREE

Dear Apple Tree,
Why does it feel
like stolen fruit?

Unconditional

Your light
is like the strings
of a marionette
activating the motionless.

Your love
is the will
of a marathon runner
increasing in speed.

You are a mender
holding needle and thread,
the first to sew
a heart cracked open.

You are the seeds
given to wild birds
liberating souls
into flight.

You are a water spring
always life-giving
flowing outward
for the ready.

COTTONWOOD

Your arms are shade patches
over the streaks
of sunlight on my counter,
a wind dance
seeping,
"I am your shelter."

RUBY

You are my morning
walk-keeper,
leash bound,
     full force
ahead, Boston Terriers
        cannot be trained
  to the left,
      wiggle
    wiggle
you set an eager pace
   carving a path
through the sand-bed,
stopping to sniff
       decay or rot,
I prefer the living;
your willpower
    when I tug
and your   thrust
toward   bolting fur
or   scuttering scales,
the flat muzzle
of yours,   grunting,
    snorting,
your forced breath
    and my crunchy
  footfall
obvious
    to the arroyo creatures.

Baking

"The Best Cookies"
recipe written on the back
of a champagne gala invitation,
a benefit for the University of Rochester
dated September, 14, 1978.
At fifteen, I wasn't their patron,
instead, the tax-deductible plea
is scrap paper
from the best part of my teens
perfected at the O'Briens
or butchered at the Browns
munchies were satiated.
The sugar was our coming home;
if they didn't greet us on racks
we prepared our own batter
too impatient for the shaping,
      raw like us
        we were undone,
each a separate ingredient
with nothing but belief
in our wholeness.

Sunday

I think of the return
of the internal
after breaking a week
of compliance,
        to pause
upon the crystal
light of morning dew
or a bird song
waking breakfast.

We experience
        our own holy,
a nurturing unbound
to dogma,
rooted in the hidden
        workings
of our souls
there is no deviance,
whether in community
        or stillness
we sense our own choosing.

GREAT HORNED OWL

Nested in a Juniper
you drop a dead rabbit
a foot from my feet,
in your fear
of my intrusion
you sacrifice your kill,
I am guilty
for your loss,
for the hardship
in your hunt
      now harder,
I feel your hunger,
awed by your escape
in silent flight
from the hills
I am borrowing.

Later in the telling
an omen
is mentioned,
the raptor transforms
from victim
      to giver
and I, once again,
      the taker
      twists the torn
      carcass
into a portent
attuned to the rare
sighting of a Strigidae
in broad daylight.

Our Knabe

Robbed of your nobility
we have silenced
you, your tonal
melody as antiqued
as the ivory keys.
My daughter's petite
fingers mimicked
notes off the page
and like a loyal horse
to its rider,
you lifted
into a sonorous proud,
        "Mignonette"
for our mignonette,
        we apologize
for your abandonment,
for your blending
into a corner wall
despite your human-carved
body and legs,
your decorative mahogany
alone and hollow.

CLOWN

Willa at six months
balanced a sippy-cup
on her head,
         no hands
with reddened cheeks
waiting for us to notice,
doubling the comedy.
She made up games
like Spider on the Bed
         or performed
Cup of Soup,
her bellowing
could turn titters
into howls.
         With deeper dimples
         she creates Pansy Pandowdy
         for Amuse Bouche,
         like a gurgling
         brook, she is an endless
         belly-flow of chuckles.

Day 21

I approach the front door
not to exit to a friend
nor to be one of the public,
merely with a full trash bag
holding tears of onions
    and its raunch,
interrupted by a centipede
    half grown
with full front pinchers,
    I want to kill.
My shoe-slam
    misses,
    zapping
the multi paired
    legs into a skitter
    zipping,
his instinct for survival
provokes my immediate
    Buddhist,
I can't end life
when the entire globe
    is in fear,
we both are metameric
    running,
my change of heart
    for a cup
to assist the arthropod
back to the stone-bed
he crawled from, the shelter
from which all beings
house their worth.

Halloween

I am Frida Kahlo
and you are Little Red Riding Hood,
we are friends
at first sight
frame and hood
only connected
by our both being in disguise
and now your mask
is a N95
        hidden
behind red silk
and polka dots
you say to brighten,
   from 6 feet
      apart,
        we talk toilet paper
          and the frugal
            way to wipe
              our asses
                clean
                  during a shortage.

TULIPS #1

I want to praise
your bolstering
from a sullen season,
yet I return my gaze
to the coarse ashen
twigs needing disposal
and the wide-open pit
                              beyond,
the same as a trench
in waiting like an open-mouth
of a corpse flower
for plywood
boxes with unclaimed Covid
            bodies
as any debris
would be swallowed,
and I despise
the thought of my garden
            beings
perhaps having received
more nurturing than these human
beings,
despite all the times I neglected
            to water
            or to talk,
my flowers were never alone.

Tulips #2

Your poppy red
goblets
shaped upon your awakening
as you open to the morning,
like you, I am pulsed
by the dawn
the chorus
of whistles and buzzes,
with petals splayed
you signal the pistil
and stamens
time for work,
no matter how hard they labor
I choose your perfection
to be in the phototropic,
our nature bent
toward the light.

MEMORY

1
Mononucleosis
the only kisses
    from visiting
grandparents

2
one month out of school
nothing to miss
      I am one
of a few thousand

3
ice cream fattens
my mom buys
    all flavors
I fantasize cookies

4
a dream of a boy
    I wake up
        tingling
naïve
    to his kind of touch

LISTENING

From a chair carved rock
nestled in a sand bed
at the foot of a limestone
cliff-side,
with a rare reminder
of this century,
the echo of rubber
to blacktop
more like the bounce
of flapping wind sails,

today's silence is ocean deep,
not the kind of quiet
upon an exit,
the stillness ripples
from an opening
where all vibrations
are sourced,
where planet earth
is heard doing the telling,
without her voice we are voiceless,
our mother's humming
is the sound of energy giving.

PUNCHING BAG

Stir crazy plants
my feet into stance,
I throw a jab
and within my first right hook
every cell in my body
        awakens
to the unexpressed,
no matter how innocent
my return,
each punch is loaded
loosening the toxic
into shaped muscle,
it doesn't matter how ancient
the history,
my flesh is a fresh
piston to the bag
softening membranes
        of stored trauma
into silk pillowcases
each blow releases the stuffing
        like goose feathers
escape through small leaks,
my core, as hard as a rock,
is no longer storage
    for stones.

Our Shelter

We are contained
           in sun-dried mud,
the adobe earth of native
soil is structured
           in Djenne
     or Arg-e Bam,
built by the Tlaxcalans
stacked by the hands
of a hippy in Cerrillos
for his parents,
in double thick bricks
committed to the authentic,
the desire to create on behalf of love
is eternal,
           devotion
are walls still standing.

EXPECTING

Upon this season, birds and buds
mingle song and citrus green
over the nakedness of limbs,
memory of leaves already pulsating
    from vein to vein,
before the camouflage
    of branches,
before the evidence of weed
or flower, anything poking
out of raw dirt
    I water,
because I know this wait,
    swollen
and ripening.

The bud inside of me preparing
its own life, my body and belly
shaped of baby about to bloom,
the soil shaped to drink
random and porous,
    I am sun and rain
housing my belief in love,
baby of patience and trust
like the trust in seasons,
the most dormant being
can be whisked
into the faith of a hidden bulb.

Witnessing a four-trunk-tree
    rotting
and leaking
roots already knowing,
the top still believing

waiving new life
    like the rest,
yet, it's a four-trunk-tree
       rotting
and leaking
as I am waiting
     swollen
and ripening
    crocuses popping,
it is thinning and rotting
while my thickening
    floods sun
and pours rain.

ANOTHER MEAL

Too much cooking
and I forget to open my heart
for flavor,
the way Nana
stood on swollen
feet all day
stirring her simmer
anticipating the mouths
of waiting baby birds,
escarole and giant meatballs
are the ingredients
but her singing
"Che bella stansalata"
while she chopped
            and patted
made it Scaloda,
she scooped love
out of bowls
the way backs are rubbed,
our second helpings
were hugs squeezing,
the leftovers brought home
helped her sleep
through the night,
we rose in the morning
hungry for our return,
for the way she served
an entire pot of food
to no matter how many guests
felt as a giving
for one.

Lost and Found

Cupped inside the white mats
of rattlesnake weed
is a fluffy cottontail
          rabbit tail,
I pluck out like a flower
claiming beauty over thorns,
the totem rabbit's downy
too airy for my calloused
hands, I feather my cheeks
hoping thinner skin
can sense the slightness
            of fur
            too fluffy
for protection,
your run could not outrun
the predator,
leaving behind detached
body parts
as gift-giving talismans,
I take you into my pocket
and feel the mass of vertebrae
press against my thigh,
you are prey captured
for the keeping of good fortune
unlike the foot rainbow-dyed
hooked on a key-chain,
          fake and gaudy
bringing me bad luck
of a mean friend,
you were not pursued
and store bought,

I accept you as a rare find
        my amulet,
as I uphold the belief
        in your rubbing.

SUNDAY DRIVE

My daughter's curtains
drawn to the street
blocking the increase
of cars perusing, the rash
of tourists are replaced
by New Mexicans, the village
as a destination now relief
from boredom, with auto
windows sealed shut
      and locked doors
        there is no strolling
through this dust devil town
absent of being greeted
with "What do you do here?"
Old fashioned smiles peer
through shatter-proof
glass, from the stories
      my mother recalls
of she and Aunt Nancy
in the backseat
with Ma in the middle
repeating Zeyer Sheyn
      Zeyer Sheyn,
everything beautiful in brief
and passing,
starring into pastures
or boulevards,
weathered-wood barns
or stone-masoned mansions,
all with the same wonder
of how they do their living,

how far the imagination
can run away from home
into the unknown,
into becoming so lost
you can trade places.

To Be Fed

Love in midair
　　twisting
as hummingbirds
　　　zipping
　　　　zipping
with lightening-sharp
　　heartbeats
　　　we are unstoppable
dancers
　　　bobbing
our aerial maneuvers
　　to pollen
　　　　flitters
　　　flitters
we hover
　　our beaks
into red blossoms
　　　to draw pollen
for high-octane
　　fuel
　　we are buzzing
　　　　buzzing
　　buzzing

Three Haikus

Lulled to sleep
t-whit tu-whoo, t-whit tu-whoo
I shall wake wiser

A vulture zips overhead
prey dangling from its mouth
I sleep scared as a mouse

The morning traffic
of chirps whittling woe and woo
drive me out of bed

For All Those

Upon this pandemic your heart opens
deeper and deeper, you are the love
keeper, like divinity
           the virus
   is a giver.
You, the keeper, the virus,
a giver.

In a brilliant flash, you return
to love, there is no bad or good
only the new levels you rise
to with what is had. The had done,
           there is no other way,
you deepen.

To know a raw day of pleading
out of suffering is the miracle,
to feel beyond the felt is hope,
           you imagine
an open iris on a blue moon,
a yellow flower turned to the sun.

Each single day is pure possibility
right down to all that is pure
           there is light,
on a new day there are new
souls stirred into the opening,
           the virus
   as giver
grounding all its keepers.

CABIN FEVER

We regress into family
time as if you were five
years old, tucked
into the pines
and earth-lit air
inside the rustic cabin
called "Golden Treasure,"
we invented a song
for, you and your cousin
giggling through the line
"It's our pleasure."
There is no measuring
our temperatures
on a three-day fishing
trip, only the trout
and the number
of times we play
What's Missing,
where time stalled
on recalling the miniature
      pink tailed mouse
      copper vase
      enamel plate,
we open our eyes
and in a hot flash
recognize the absent
      red hammer.

DISPLACED

My husband warns
of black widows
under the stone bench,
I think of the homeless
and all their spider bites
    all the venom
waiting in cool
dark places,
    all the places
they are displaced
from, the shelters
during shortages
with less volunteers
with less food
for their cooking,
    there is less
for the "Less fortunate,"
infinitely more spinnerets
are threading sticky webs
claiming benches
as their home.

Home Improvement

We think it's about
the paint,
the swatches
    of color
which will brighten
    the most,
or the entrance doors,
made of etched glass
    and worn steel,
a material we can anticipate
with; the aging of rust
into a patina,
we speak in tongues
attempting to translate
    "Fawn Brindle"
or "Silken Peacock,"
it doesn't matter
what we settle,
there's always the discussion
of another room.

Afterword

Poem for a Poet
For Cari from Gary (Glazner)

Do you have a shovel?
And a shoulder?
Because it's time to get digging.
Our main shoveler has been working overtime.
Each day for 31 days, she dug into the earth.
Each day for 31 days, she put her sweet shoulder to the grindstone.
Digging for poems is hard work people!
While Leonard Cohen may say,
"I'm just paying my rent every day in the Tower of Song."
And Wee Willie Shakeshake may bake more than birds
in Titus Andronicus, into his sweet/sweetie pies,
as we all chant:
Sing a song of sixpence,
A pocket full of rye.
Four and twenty blackbirds,
Baked in a pie.
Look people- Mama ain't been singing, she been
digging for all our rents in arrears.
She been all up in our noses with the poetic
and the proses.
She dug a hole so deep all the sheep began to beep!
Like beep, beep get out of my way suckers!
I'm trying to dig a hole to the future.
Dig a poetic hole to jump in.
She say, get you in my fox hole poetry people.
Dearest Cari, you have carried us to the finish line.
Like EE Cummings, you have carried our hearts in your heart.
We the people of Planet Adobe Brick, say thank you!
Thanks for all the poems past and poems to come.
Thanks for being our tireless poetry worker.

Thanks for helping us pay the terrible rent due,
for all the folks that have lost life
or loved ones to this godforsaken virus.
The ones left standing will offer up poems
disguised as a prayer, as we toss that shovel
of sacred red earth on the graves
of those remembered souls.

"Expectation, more dangerous than any blade."
Tess Gallagher

"Memory becomes the exercise against loss."
Ruth Stone

BEFORE THE CONTAGIOUS

APATHY

When you hear the word war
it should be the image
of your child falling backwards
off a jungle-gym, the sound of
his head slamming onto concrete
like the slap of a hardbound
dictionary hitting a stone floor straight-up.

When you see the word war
you should startle, your body
shake, scream for help
the way you would for your child,
seeing them flat-out
anticipating the damage,
something has to be wrong
while he is lying too still
before the rumble of tears,
something has to be wrong.

When you feel the word war
the headache your child tells
you he has should transfer to your head,
travel to your stomach and quake
with or without your own experiences
his pain alone is your pain,
while you fear the worst
their war is your war.

Waiting for the war
is watching over this child
for a concussion,
checking the size of his pupils
or dizziness or fatigue,

the possibility of brain-damage
like the brain-damaged
decision of war,
the brain-damaged decision of war.

December 26th, 2004

The day the tsunami hit
my three year old daughter was thrown
into the ocean,
entered for the first time
by her uncle's tossing
because she said, "Yes" to the word toss,
and he childless, thought she understood.
When the vest sprung her to the surface
her face mimicked the face
of another child across the world, another ocean
where the force of a salt-block
slams him under for the first gulp.
The same eyes predominate
on my child or her child,
the punctured hollow between their sockets
darkened into the ripples
of their foreheads, cascading
down to cheekbones,
the inflated iris's blacken
a straight beam toward both mothers,
yet I am calm in a boat floating
when my child is plopped
into my lap.
My hand caresses as her metacarpals
clamp onto her child's arm,
his fear unbearable as soon as I sooth my daughter's,
her shaking underneath a life-jacket
melding into my sun-spots,
my love doing the sweltering
as his life is underneath naked
shivering pleas to his mother
while he wails for a lap she cannot flatten,
           a second gulp

as I watch my daughter blink away the stinging
his mother cannot blindfold
           her love impotent,
a mother's love impotent.
While my daughter calms, her quivering lips
intermittent like the slow last movements
of a wind-up toy, inside the brief seconds
before stillness,
           they say it takes three,
the terror stops, the five hundred
mile-an-hour thrashing is as placid as the fiberglass
my child and I rock in, her child takes in water
like air and she knows his organs fill smoothly,
with less pain than her first hit of nicotine,
with no pain to the lifetime of a mother's sorrow.

THIN SKINNED

Talking to my thirteen year old daughter
is like picking mulberries,
the gentle approach, finger tips-tip
toward the berry, prongs for the prize,
the soft round words prime her ears,
both are framed, then the pull
toward the taker, tugging the fused
carpels, squeezing them away while whole,
breaking her away, unbroken.
Even the mouth knows how useless one bundle
of nutlets is, one sentence shapes nothing,
                              keep pulling,
sense the firm fruit, find the give, reject
the swollen ripe,
emotions overdone splattering
on garments overpurchased.

There is no way to avoid stain,
youth's memory is mulberry-purple
dye to cotton,
to cook something up; more is needed,
past the outreaching limbs
into the center, twelve pies are born,
                    six of her lies
                    six of my myths,
                    all twelve die.
Soap on my fingers drips away the color of ink,
she will remember the hug,
the basket full
and how we added sugar.

CANDYBOWL

Emily Post could not tame
the little hand grasping
for chocolates candies,
there is no finger-picking;
the full bundle tuck
and a wavering tongue.

NUTS

Cracked open or up
proteined or crazed
harvested or labeled,
if I am nuts, I am tree-born
limb hung, coveted
or squandered,
human bound, roasted, salted,
cupped into a hand,
and never alone, companion
taps into companion
before rolling onto the tongue
of a stranger.

If I am nuts, you must break
my shell, have a tool
stronger than your own grip,
and the will of your teeth
to expose me out of my house,
my meat a soft nectar
as you prefer to crunch and chomp.

If I am nuts, I am not your snack,
I am your allergen,
your anaphylactic shock.

PRAISE THE LORD

Praise the Lord when a bus
full of good Christians, a full Baptist
choir singing his praises
crashes, praise the Lord,
eight die, more injured for life.

Praise the Lord, you slammed
your head and was told surgery
or die, surgeon's hands peeled
flesh from skull like an orange rind,
your hard-headedness turns to hard
cranium cracking
into a miracle sucking out the clot.
You never sang his praises.

Praise the Lord, blood
on the bus, bone split bone,
praise him when they live, praise
him when they die. I pray beyond all names,
                              beyond faith invented
to beliefs outside of myself
I am damned because of their salvation.

Praise the Lord, three little boys
die on their way to school, bullets
popping easier than popcorn,
              bullets popping
                    easier than popcorn,
praise the Lord, a toddler girl lives
after her meth mom's neglect, food
down to ketchup packets, curled up in a dry bathtub
                    she lives, they die.
Whose miracle is whose? Duck, duck
goooooooose.

Praise the Lord, that your sins
are righteous enough to be forgiven
that I am goodness while tapping
heads and shrilling, duck, duck, duck
                    duck, duck
allow me to be praiseworthy
when I giggle, goooooooooose,
praise the Lord, your turn to live
your turn to die.

SWIMMER

You dip in with a dolphin nose
fleshed and finned
a slick skimmer
over landless jello,
a blow-up floaty bobbing.
You're a play-toy
with a pull string
stroking in butterfly,
you flit over the deep deep
as if the ocean were surface deep,
one big bright yellow daisy.

You dunk in with plastic eyes
wide open fully under, pushing
forward in breaststroke
the gurgling gurgles
could be milk sucking,
your mouth sealed to float
belly to water womb. A gulp
of air snaps you to the surface
as you are in guest status,
your face re-immerses
the way you ran
to your best friend's house,
and twists for air
again as if hearing the dinner bell.
Run, run.
Ring, ring.

In a past life you were a desert
riverbed, bone-dry
ground bound,
and this life

every pore craves the quenching.
You dream with breath through gills
to tongue, the way one speaks
a forgotten language fluently
in their sleep,
non recordo
si sono timido,
non record
si sono timido.
Run, run.
Ring, ring.
Go back, it's not time yet.
Go back until you deserve your death.
Swim into your tunnel of light.

Cello Solo, to the Soul

What would you think
if in every corner of the room
there was a side of yourself
staring back at you, your heart
broken to the east, your spirit
levitating to the west, a tantric
brainwave to the south,
muscles flexing to the north?
If every day started with seizing
the leftovers of your past,
the catapult in pain,
the relief in forgiveness,
your breath exchanging inhale
to exhale coherently,
flowing in are the questions
to keep you open.
You are a wild cat on the couch,
a hawk on the chandelier,
a snake in the fireplace,
a dolphin in the fishbowl.
In every direction a version
peers into yourself, a full on garden
in peak bloom, you as a sunflower
the tallest, your face the seeds
facing daylight
until there is nothing left
but to sleep.

GIVING THANKS

Words of the other thirteen
over the scraping
of my Nana's silver
onto Grandpa Rabin's china
tap tap family
clink clink health,
and I want to be Polly Anna
having mashed the potatoes
without seeing politicians
between the grates,
mashing for the sake of mashing
without anger slamming
the masher to the bottom
splattering potatoes.
Polly adds butter
and whips in the milk
                tap tap family
                clink clink health,
I want her bow and ruffles
so I can apply frosted lipstick
without knowing what my car
burned on the way to my sister's
                tap tap family
                clink clink health.

I want to be Polly Anna
because I can't be my mother's
mother, whom, when asked
what she was thankful for, pounded
her fist on the table
and said, "Not a goddamn thing"
                tap tap family
                clink clink health,

la di da da da
I don't know what to do
with my uhhhhh
please help me with la di da,
          tap tap family
            clink clink health.
I want to be Polly Anna
because she loves her family.
I want to be Polly Anna
because she loves her work,
          tap tap family
            clink clink health.
I want to be her because she loves
her life and she's happy
       with a smile
             all of the time,
she is free with no idea
people feel trapped,
I want to be Polly Anna
because she is free
from freedom,
....and I am thankful,
tap tap family
clink clink health.

Leaf

Leaf on an autumn trip
      spinning
          spinning

Love like daybreak
      believing
          believing

For Joseph Henry Sharp's Aspens in Hondo Canon, Near Twining

Sidetrack any heartache
onto the narrow path
nestled into the small season
of aspen turning, trudging
leaden feet higher into brilliant
yellow, the color of distant sun,
its light tinges tips of wavering leaves
tingling into you a respite,
you levitate into the spark
to take shelter under the canopy
of leaf glow, the slim trunks
are peels of chalky mica sheets,
each individual tree a petite pearl
amid the glittering cluster
strung like a necklace,
to be in awe of its jeweler.

HOLY WATER

I'd like to borrow your faith
      in holy water.
Go down to where I'm dirtiest,
drop past all the lingo,
way past the lingo of low self-esteem,
that "Not good enough" voice
hunching shoulders, apologizing
for being in the same room,
down,
down to where thinking out of religion goes.
Down, down to, "It wasn't my fault."
Down, down to where your sin
is my sin,
      I'm a sin-mixer,
into your holy water.
I'll buy it Catholic for forty dollars a bottle,
holy cross prayers as my prayers,
      I'm a prayer-mixer.
Throw Rosh Hashanah bread
into your Jewish water,
and watch it bloat.
You can have my feet
ankles down, elbows down to hands,
take my mouth,
extra water enter my mouth,
especially the mouth,
five times a day for Wudu,
I'd like to borrow your faith
      in holy water
after the cleansing.

To drink an entire cup of Nam Mon
every morning, its magic

to keep me clean,
let me hold the candle for wax
drippings in the alms bowl,
floating gold leaves and lotuses,
your holiness
             is my holiness.
Drop me into your Hindu, wash my grime
in the Ganges River, so I may
be sacred before I pray,
             I'm a prayer-mixer
waiting for the high-priest at Menik Ganga
to do the water cutting ceremony,
             I'm a water-cutter,
running naked chanting for holy spots
in the Sri Lanka's river.
I'd like to borrow your faith
             in holy water.
To be dunked and then popped
out of a human tank, as if bursting
away from the placenta, new-born,
             I'm a born-again.

Your sin is my sin,
             I'm a sin-mixer.
Pray for me with your prayers
or your belief's prayers,
I'll take all prayers
and scrub them into the holy water
right down to the bones
of all religions,
scrub down to all their storytellers,
deep down to the sins
in their stories.
Holy water,
             take me down.

PREMONITION

She slept too close
to her dream
and woke up
believing (with a prayer)
she could be
someone else
if no one else
was looking.

TIMING

She caught herself
running fast
in the wrong direction
                    startled
by her reflection
in the glass
                if broken
her heart could open
wider than the mystery of love,
love
which could be let go of
                    or lost
to see it better.

Rollover

The reminder of death
on a breath giving spring day
shocks the celebration of my daughter's birth
pushes purple tulips into the shade
for black.
Our car does its duty
humming its way down the highway,
the girls, one in a white daisy dress,
with giggles like toots.
My husband's wrist rests over the top of the wheel
and steers with a dangling hand, a few veins
and thin flesh keeps tires between yellow
lines. I am dreamy,
my head pulled to the mountains
for the raw green upon ripe green.

"Stop the car." "Let me out."
By the time he stops, I need to sprint.
The flipped car in the distance is helpless
like a beetle on its back,
tires free spinning like tarsi wiggling
but I run toward the people
who are going to need more than fingertips
to turn spindle legs right side up; *there must be people.*
I run ahead of my body, past my kettle-drum
heart, a pair of skates without the speed skater
I'm sizeless yet inflating.
           Where are the helpers?
When I see a couple men they are like inflatable air dancers
bobbing with wonky fingers pointing.

Molded into the sand of San Felipe Pueblo
she's my girl's age in a few years, protruding

as if left there by excavation,
half unearthed, intact but smothered in sacred dirt,
her eyes pop open to prove the miracle, the whites clean
against her smudged face, and she asks for her boyfriend.
   Where are the helpers?
The men's screams are fueled, "Not in the car,
no one's in the car." From the sand juts along the steel's
rim, two little feet protrude, his feet in blue tennis shoes,
there is no ruby-red sticking out from under, a boy
pressed under, not a wicked witch.
We whoosh to his head side of the car where Native
American men have appeared, blown-up animated
muscle men, all at once charging, "Lift."
Shrilling above, "Lift," is the lone squeal of, "No,"
from a thin too groomed man.
"Lift," "No," a booming, "Lift," "Nohoh,
unless you want to see blood and guts."

My bird bones join elephant trunks, will to will, five-thousand
pounds is air entering air, air-bound
the stampede slams the car rubber down, they herd past the firm
wheels into the man-made dust devil, yet I am planted
where my six-inch slice of pushing occurred
and there, touching my big toe, is a head
of raven black hair, where he could have been trampled,
my little spot, a blind spot in waiting. "Nohoh,
blood and guts."
   Where are the helpers?
I drop down to the boy more like a rubber band
doll twisted and toyed,
I am the helper, "No," claims the blood and guts man,
there is blood, blood is the only thing lively,
a red river flowing out of his mouth where exhale
should live. There are gawkers shrilling death

as I drape my essence above him like a white cloak
blocking him from the hysterics, I plead, "Breath."

My hand caresses his forehead as if he were my own,
the blood of my own could never be gruesome, his body
now as invisible as hidden under the car, soul to soul
I love him, he is not injured amid the love I feel, "Breath."
This compassion is not mine, but surrounds me and is given,
travels down from the tunnel which could have taken,
I have traveled down from the tunnel, the light forced
back into my empty shell twenty years ago is this boy's light.
"Breathe," I scream over the fear of the blood and guts
people, twice the love blurs out their human forms
into pure pulse, independent of flesh, from love unattached
"I love you son," "Breath." I am the helper, for you I have stolen
love from love, light from light,
"Caawww, caaawww," like a crow to dawn,
his ribcage crackles open. He wheezes his first words,
"Mohhm." He re-enters attached to her, "Mohhmm,"
as if from the birth-bed, the relief felt from his first cry
outside of her womb, returns.

Gentle Husband

Rain to earth, we are soul-match
to soul-match, pitter-patter
                    pitter-patter,
reminding me of the thirst
before we met,
you showed up in the nick,
our first touch, a lightening
bolt up my arm blows
your cover. You are naked
next to my past.

Before you, I cloaked
my men, splashed
them in Pollack paint,
how unadorned our love
is, rooted underground,
will to will, from dirt below
we clean the surface,
will to will, we are code-talkers,
unearthing secrets
through thunder,
we are window closers
            and door keepers,
                    opening
                    opening.

Almost

He shuts the door
to leave behind
her jumbled words

feeling her sincerity

several blocks away
closer to this beauty.

Thanksgiving

1

When I went to sleep
half in half out,
my fingers stretched like silly
putty, all the way to the brightest
star, shining like a planet, probably
Venus, my flesh-tip
not commanding a wish,
too grateful for the journey.

2

He gave her flowers
taller than the year
before, the scent bred
out for nursing homes
and restaurants, yet the ruby
red was pungent
and she was thankful.

3

She's three-and-a-half this holiday,
three-and-a-half cups of cooked
squash I try to scoop
without breaking the shell,
her spoon forces
its way into the nubbed bowl,
my perfection does not want her help
and then I remember,
these days go quick.
The scent of cinnamon
usually sprinkled over her oatmeal,
she giggles at the seeds
the way she laughs at my dancing.

She takes petite teaspoons of pulp
out of the turbine rind for serving dish
with a few pokes and cracks later, we are mother
and toddler cooking.

4
I could explode
into a prayer
for all of the flaws
of the world,
but this table is too rich,
red leaves and uncracked nuts,
candles and clementines
stilling any house
outside of mine,
and for a brief moment
my heart too full, its love
unsuspicious.

5
Peace is as radiant
as the desire in this room.

6:00 News

He used a kitchen knife to cut off her head,
and I am in the kitchen using a knife
to cut florets off a broccoli head.
He used a kitchen knife to cut off her head,
precisely, I cut to leave an inch of stalk
below the emerald green bunches,
he used a kitchen knife to cut off her head.

I sip some wine anticipating a good meal,
he used a kitchen knife to cut off her head,
chopping the stalks into half inches,
        crunch
          crunch
he used a kitchen knife to cut off her head,
red wine drips down the side of my glass,
did he notice the color of her hair
before her blood?

He used a kitchen knife to cut off her head,
had she eaten her last meal alone?
My sharpest knife is used for onions, the quicker
I chop shortens the burning of my eyes,
did he select the blade,
or pace his speed,
or want her death?
I slice the Vidalia in half, then in thin slices,
what was sliced away from him in order to do the slicing?
He used a kitchen knife to cut off her head.
Tears flood down my cheeks
        chop
          chop
with blurred vision I tip the wineglass,
red pooling over white tiles

in my kitchen, her blood running under the dinner table
in her kitchen, he used a kitchen knife to cut off her head.

Lot Number 8

This is the backyard
of your backyard
      and any yard
fenced in to be mine.
Winter persuaded
by ripe avocado green,
the chirping birds
awakening our own voices
to the trees, trees
planted within a property line,
roots entangled over the line.
Sun shines on the tip
of my branches, above your roof,
illuminating gaps
between the wired wood
dividing us, large enough
for a garner snake
having just eaten to slip
through into your yard
to across the street
     in their yard
         never to be back.

Purple flax in her garden,
she chooses flowers
with seeds that can travel,
can be up-winded
to become the jewels
of nearby caretakers
unlike the petunias
prim for a season
for container pots,
as found in my plot

patted into glazed ceramic
for the deck,
where I watch the view
of sunsets lit next door,
or in the distance,
sangre from the foothills
drips over tin pitched
                    mansions,
magenta across the street
turns darker now in your yard
darkening the slits forming fence
into a dense hue
until there is no ground,
until all is lost and upward
there is no his, hers, or mine.
The first bright star
silencing the voices
which repeat
I wish I may, I wish I might
                    from anywhere,
vorrei poter, vorrei se potessi,
                         anywhere,
I wish I may, I wish I might,
vorrei poter, vorrei se potessi.

DIPTYCH

The snail-paced-doer
and soft-thinker
can't see their own life
in front of reality TV,
too tired from a day
they hated
too exhausted to think
out of it, sunken
into the couch.
The wind chops
into the hollyhocks,
the flowers behind the den
wall, the gust slams
through the bee's dinner
thrusts them to and fro'
as easily as pharmaceuticals
slide down the snail-paced-doer
and soft-thinker's throat.
These Hawaiian imposters
pricked by whisking dirt
from the desert floor,
the snail-paced-doer
and soft-thinker
bezeled to the weather
yet, undisturbed by the bellowing,
the delay of heat
stalling a moment between season,
the intention between clasp and link.
The tall pillars
too tropical above gray stones,
the snail-paced doer
and soft-thinker
need to get up

into the forced air
like the misplaced flower bolts,
their vibrancy amid prickly pear
offers grace.
The snail-paced-doer
and soft-thinker
need to stand
within the grove of stalks
and garnish,
riveting and tilting
alongside them, the gale
forced into the fibers,
to feel for themselves
a beauty which is both malleable
and resilient.

UNWRAP

1

I Knew someone who was born
on Christ's birthday, but his parents
found this inconvenient so they changed
his birthday to January 25th,
in order to celebrate the birth
of baby Jesus uninterrupted.

2

We always had room
for one more at our Sicilian
Christmas buffet,
one more,
        and one more…….
until most of our friends
knew why it took us so long
to eat.

3

She fantasized about
spending less time
shopping this year, imagining
she would cook a turkey
for the family
she always wanted to adopt.

4

At five he calculated
how good to be,
but when he sat
on Santa's lap
he couldn't recite
his "good boy" list,

feeling all he really wanted
for Christmas
was to go home.

5
He asked her to close
her eyes, but when she
opened her hands
they were still empty,
despite the shimmering.

6
Nana's nubby fingers
and uneven knuckles
shaped perfect Christmas cookies,
crunchy butter aftertaste,
icing thickly sweet,
every single one made
for someone else.

7
What does she give him,
the person that never looked
when she pointed
out the first morning-light
pumping dew drops
on naked branches?

Homecoming

You arrive like the rise of morning,
shadow fused to fire,
a promise towards the light
igniting the heart open
to the color of beauty;
as in the flesh
of a blood orange alluring
one to its pulp,
you are the enticement
for the juice.
    Awakening one before the glare
to a sky which can be stared
into, chakra magenta beams
as the peace found in meditation.
I do not oversleep
you, a blade of grass
gleaming dew, you are the dew
to all blades,
one shimmering crystal.

For Leon Kroll's Santa Fe Hills

At first glance hovering the foothills
a slice of dulled daylight azure
sandwiched between cumulus
clouds for angels
and the night-sky rushing
to thicken a thunderstorm,
his family as dramatic as the land
which captures him, he pauses
to admire what really brings him home;
his daughter carrying buckets of water
carefully for her mother, his wife's red
hands raw against her winter-wash
forearms, remnants of light streak her hair
bouncing off of dull brown are fire threads
the way iron highlights the clay earth,
he feels the silk strands over his calluses.
She waits for him as patience
for rain in a thriving high desert
and his missing her is desperate craving
as thirsty as brittle buffalo grass,
through the whisking air he shall embrace
her the same way turbulence
delivers both fuel and beauty.

About the Author

Cari Griffo resides in the dusty old mining town Cerrillos, NM, outside of Santa Fe. She has written several screenplays and the pilot "Canyon Road," streaming on Amazon Prime. Cari has performed many of her poems in Before The Contagious to a live audience. This is her second poetry book.